PLAIN ENGLISH
FOR LAWYERS

Second Edition

PLAIN ENGLISH FOR LAWYERS

Second Edition

Richard C. Wydick
Professor of Law
University of California, Davis

1985
Carolina Academic Press
Durham, North Carolina

L.C.C. Card No. 85–70719
ISBN: 0–89089–251–2 (cloth)
ISBN: 0–89089–256–3 (paper)

Carolina Academic Press
P.O. Box 8795, Forest Hills Station
Durham, North Carolina 27707

To JJW, with love.

CONTENTS

PREFACE

The second edition of *Plain English for Lawyers*, like the first edition, is intended to help lawyers and law students learn how to express themselves in a clear, simple style. The premise of this book is that legal writing should not differ (without good reason) from ordinary, well-written English.

This second edition contains more exercises to help readers practice what they have read. The format and organization have been improved. Some portions of the first edition proved to contain bad advice, or useless advice, and those portions have been deleted. New material has been added concerning sentence structure, multiple negatives, and a peculiar lawyerism that is dubbed "cosmic detachment."

The author and the publisher are gratified by the wide acceptance of *Plain English for Lawyers* in law schools and in the legal profession. The hope for better legal writing is likely to be realized by the current generation of lawyers.

ACKNOWLEDGEMENTS

The first edition of *Plain English for Lawyers* was a revised version of an article that appeared in 66 California Law Review 727, published by the students of the University of California, Berkeley, School of Law, copyright 1978, by the California Law Review, Inc.

I wish to thank my colleagues, Margaret Johns and Raymond Parnas, who made helpful suggestions for the second edition. I am especially indebted to Robert Maddock of Davis, California, who is responsible for the cover and design of the second edition.

Richard C. Wydick
Davis, California
March, 1985

PLAIN ENGLISH
FOR LAWYERS

Second Edition

CHAPTER ONE

Why Plain English

We lawyers cannot write plain English. We use eight words to say what could be said in two. We use arcane phrases to express commonplace ideas. Seeking to be precise, we become redundant. Seeking to be cautious, we become verbose. Our sentences twist on, phrase within clause within clause, glazing the eyes and numbing the minds of our readers. The result is a writing style that has, according to one critic, four outstanding characteristics. It is: "(1) wordy, (2) unclear, (3) pompous, and (4) dull."[1]

Criticism of lawyers' writing is nothing new. In 1596, an English chancellor decided to make an example of a particularly prolix document filed in his court. The chancellor first ordered a hole cut through the center of the document, all 120 pages of it. Then he ordered that the person who wrote it should have his head stuffed through the hole, and the unfortunate fellow was led around to be exhibited to all those attending court at Westminster Hall.[2]

When the common law was transplanted to America, the writing style of the old English lawyers came with it. In 1817 Thomas Jefferson lamented that in drafting statutes his fellow lawyers were accustomed to "making every other word a 'said' or 'aforesaid', and saying everything over two or three times, so that nobody but we of the craft can untwist the diction and find out what it means. . . ."[3]

In the 1970's, criticism of legal writing took on a new intensity. The popular press castigated lawyers for the frustration and outrage that consumers feel when trying to puzzle through an insurance policy, an installment loan agreement, or an income tax instruction booklet. Even lawyers became critics.[4] For instance, one lawyer charged that in writing as we do, we "unnecessarily mystify our work, baffle our clients, and alienate the public."[5]

More recent years have brought some progress toward reform. A number of states have adopted "Plain English Laws" that require some kinds of consumer documents to be clear and concise.[6] Many good legal writing books have appeared.[7] Some judges have started crafting their opinions with greater care, and some lawyers have changed the style in which they write legal briefs. Good law schools have begun to stress simplicity and clarity in their legal writing courses.

Yet much remains to be done. If you do not believe it, walk to the nearest law library, pick any recent book at random, open to any page, and read.

The need for change is magnified by innovations in the mechanics of lawyering. Word processors can now type old boilerplate at a thousand words a minute. Computer research systems can spew forth all the writings of appellate courts, legislatures, and governmental agencies. Unless we change, we may drown in our own bad prose.

A well-known New York lawyer tells the young associates in his firm that good legal writing does not sound as though it had been written by a lawyer. In short, good legal writing is plain English. Here is an example of plain English, the statement of facts from the majority opinion in *Palsgraf v. Long Island Railroad Co.*,[8] written by Benjamin Cardozo:

> Plaintiff was standing on a platform of defendant's railroad after buying a ticket to go to Rockaway Beach. A train stopped at the station, bound for another place. Two men ran forward to catch it. One of the men reached the platform of the car without mishap, though the train was already moving. The other man, carrying a package, jumped aboard the car, but seemed unsteady as if about to fall. A guard on the car, who had held the door open, reached forward to help him in, and another guard on the platform pushed him from behind. In this act, the package was dislodged and fell upon the rails. It was a package of small size, about fifteen inches long, and was covered by newspaper. In fact it contained fireworks, but there was nothing in its appearance to give notice of its contents. The fireworks when they fell exploded. The shock of the explosion threw down some scales at the other end of the platform many feet away. The scales struck the plaintiff, causing injuries for which she sues.

What distinguishes the writing style in this passage from that found in most legal writing? Notice Justice Cardozo's economy of words. He does not say "*despite the fact that* the train was already moving" — he says "*though* the train was already moving."

Notice his choice of words. There are no archaic, lawyerly phrases, no misty abstractions, no *hereinbefores*.

Notice his care in arranging words. There are no wide gaps between the subjects and their verbs, nor between the verbs and their objects. There are no ambiguities to leave us wondering who did what to whom.

Notice his use of verbs. Most of them are in the simple form, and all but two are in the active voice.

Notice the length and construction of his sentences. Most of them contain only one main thought, and they vary in length: the shortest is six words, and the longest is twenty-seven words.

These and other elements of plain English style are discussed in this book. But you cannot learn to write plain English by reading a book. You must put your own pencil to paper. That is why practice exercises are included at the end of each section. When you finish the section, work the exercises. Then compare your results with those suggested in Appendix I at the end of the book. You will find additional exercises in Appendix II.

CHAPTER TWO

Omit Surplus Words

As a beginning lawyer, I was assigned to assist an older man, a business litigator. He hated verbosity. When I would bring him what I thought was a finished piece of work, he would read it quietly and take out his pen. As I watched over his shoulder, he would strike out whole lines, turn clauses into phrases, and turn phrases into single words. One day at lunch, I asked him how he did it. He shrugged and said: "It's not hard — just omit the surplus words."

How to Spot Bad Construction

In every English sentence are two kinds of words: working words and glue words. The working words carry the meaning of the sentence. In the preceding sentence the working words are these: *working, words, carry, meaning,* and *sentence.* The others are glue words: *the, the, of,* and *the.* The glue words do perform a vital service. They hold the working words together to form a proper, grammatical sentence. Without them, the sentence would read like a telegram. But if the *proportion* of glue words is too high, that is a symptom of a badly constructed sentence.

A well-constructed sentence is like fine cabinetwork. The pieces are cut and shaped to fit together with scarcely any glue. When you find too many glue words in a sentence, take it apart and reshape the pieces to fit together tighter. Consider this example:

> A trial by jury was requested by the defendant.

If the working words are underlined the sentence looks like this:

> A <u>trial</u> by <u>jury</u> was <u>requested</u> by the <u>defendant</u>.

Five words in that nine-word sentence are glue: *a, by, was, by,* and *the.*

How can we say the same thing in a tighter sentence with less glue? First, move *defendant* to the front and make it the subject of the sentence. Second, use *jury trial* in place of *trial by jury.* The sentence would thus read:

> The defendant requested a jury trial.

If the working words are underlined, the rewritten sentence looks like this:

> The <u>defendant</u> <u>requested</u> a <u>jury</u> <u>trial</u>.

Again there are four working words, but the glue words have been cut from five to two. The sentence means the same as the original, but it is tighter and one-third shorter.

Here is another example:

> The ruling by the trial judge was prejudicial error for the reason that it cut off cross-examination with respect to issues that were vital.

If the working words are underlined, we have:

> The <u>ruling</u> by the <u>trial judge</u> was <u>prejudicial</u> error for the
> <u>reason</u> that it <u>cut off</u> <u>cross-examination</u> with respect to
> <u>issues</u> that were <u>vital</u>.

In a sentence of twenty-four words, eleven carry the meaning and thirteen are glue.

Note the string of words *the ruling by the trial judge*. That tells us that it was the trial judge's ruling. Why not just say *the trial judge's ruling*? The same treatment will tighten the words at the end of the sentence. *Issues that were vital* tells us that they were vital issues. Why not say *vital issues*? Now note the phrase *for the reason that*. Does it say any more than *because*? If not, we can use one word in place of four. Likewise, *with respect to* can be reduced to *on*. Rewritten, the sentence looks like this:

> The trial judge's ruling was prejudicial error because it
> cut off cross-examination on vital issues.

Here it is with the working words underlined:

> The <u>trial judge's</u> <u>ruling</u> was <u>prejudicial</u> <u>error</u> because it
> <u>cut</u> <u>off</u> <u>cross-examination</u> on <u>vital</u> <u>issues</u>.

The revised sentence uses fifteen words in place of the original twenty-four, and eleven of the fifteen are working words. The sentence is both tighter and stronger than the original.

Consider a third example, but this time use a pencil and paper to rewrite the sentence yourself.

> In many instances, insofar as the jurors are concerned,
> the jury instructions are not understandable because they
> are too poorly written.

Does your sentence trim the phrase *in many instances*? Here the single word *often* will suffice. Does your sentence omit the phrase *insofar as the jurors are concerned*? That adds bulk but no meaning. Finally, did you find a way to omit the clumsy *because* clause at the end of the sentence? Your rewritten sentence should look something like this:

> Often jury instructions are too poorly written for the jurors to understand.

Here it is with the working words underlined:

> Often <u>jury</u> <u>instructions</u> <u>are</u> <u>too</u> <u>poorly</u> <u>written</u> for the <u>jurors</u> to <u>understand</u>.

The rewritten sentence is nine words shorter than the original, and nine of its twelve words are working words.

Exercise 1

Underline the working words in the sentences below. Note the proportion of glue words to working words. Then rewrite the sentences, underline the working words, and compare your results with the original sentences.

1. The <u>testimony</u> that was <u>given</u> by <u>Reeves</u> went to the heart of the <u>defense</u> that he <u>asserted</u>, which was his <u>lack</u> of the <u>specific intent</u> to <u>escape</u>.

2. In the <u>event</u> that there is a <u>waiver</u> of the <u>attorney-client privilege</u> by the <u>client</u>, the <u>letters</u> must be <u>produced</u> by the <u>attorney</u> for the <u>purpose</u> of <u>inspection</u> by the <u>adversary party</u>.

Answers on page 77. More exercises on page 89.

Avoid Compound Constructions

Compound constructions (such as compound prepositions) use three or four words to do the work of one or two words. They suck the vital juices from your writing. You saw some examples in the last section. *With respect to* was used instead of *on*. *For the reason that* was used instead of *because*.

Every time you see one of these pests on your page, swat it. Use a simple form instead. Here is a list of examples:

Compound	Simple
at that point in time	then
by means of	by
by reason of	because of
by virtue of	by, under
for the purpose of	to
for the reason that	because
in accordance with	by, under
inasmuch as	since
in connection with	with, about, concerning
in favor of	for
in order to	to
in relation to	about, concerning
in the event that	if
in the nature of	like
prior to	before
subsequent to	after
with a view to	to
with reference to	about, concerning

Exercise 2

Use one or two words to replace the compound constructions in these sentences.

1. The parties were in complete agreement ~~with respect to~~ *(about)* the amount of rent due and also ~~as regards~~ *(about)* the due date.
2. ~~From the point of view of~~ *(For)* simplicity, an ordinary deed of trust would be the best.
3. ~~On the basis of~~ *(Because of)* the *Burke* decision, the savings clause was added ~~for the purpose of~~ *(to)* avoiding any ambiguity.
4. ~~In terms of~~ *(In considering)* fairness, we should not apply the new rule retroactively.
5. When the funds are received, we will transfer title ~~with the thought in mind of~~ *(hoping to)* clearing up all questions ~~as respects~~ *(about)* this matter.
6. ~~At this point in time,~~ *(Here)* I cannot recall what the letter was ~~with regard to.~~ *(about)*

Answers on page 78. More exercises on page 90.

Avoid Word-Wasting Idioms

Once you develop a distaste for surplus words, you will find many word-wasting idioms that can be

trimmed from your sentences with no loss of meaning.
For instance:

> The fact that the defendant was young may have influenced the jury.

What meaning does *the fact that* add? Why not say:

> The defendant's youth may have influenced the jury.

The fact that is almost always surplus. See how it can be trimmed from these examples:

Verbose	Concise
the fact that she had died	her death
he was aware of the fact that	he knew
despite the fact that	although, even though
because of the fact that	because

Likewise, words like *case, instance,* and *situation* spawn verbosity:

Verbose	Concise
in some instances the parties can	sometimes the parties can
in many cases you will find	often you will find
that was a situation in which the court	there the court

RICO claims are now more fre-quent than was formerly the case	RICO claims are more frequent now
injunctive relief is required in the situation in which	injunctive relief is required when
in the majority of instances the grantor	usually the grantor

Other examples of common word-wasting idioms that you can eliminate with no loss of meaning are:

Verbose	**Concise**
during the time that	during, while
for the period of	for
insofar as . . . is concerned	(omit it and start with the subject)
there is no doubt but that	doubtless, no doubt
the question as to whether	whether, the ques-tion whether
this is a topic that	this topic
until such time as	until

Exercise 3

Revise these examples to omit the word-wasting idioms.

1. At such time as the judgment is entered . . .
2. This is a situation in which estoppel can be invoked . . .
3. He was sentenced to the county jail for a period of five months . . .
4. Pursuant to the terms of our contract . . .
5. There can be no doubt but that the statute applies to the situation in which . . .
6. The claim was clarified by means of a bill of particulars . . .
7. The trial judge must consider the question as to whether . . .
8. This offer will stand until such time as you . . .
9. In most instances the claimant's good faith is not disputed . . .
10. The plaintiff filed the complaint despite the fact that she knew . . .
11. Arbitration is useful in some instances in which the parties . . .
12. This is a point that has troubled many courts . . .
13. Because of the fact that he was injured . . .

Answers on page 79. More exercises on page 91.

Focus on the Actor, the Action, and the Object

One way to remedy a wordy, fog-bound sentence is to ask yourself: "Who is doing what to whom in this sentence?"[9] Then rewrite the sentence to focus on those three key elements — the actor, the action, and the object of the action. First, state the actor. Then state the action, using the strongest verb that will fit. Last, state the object of the action. Here is a simple example:

It is possible for the court to modify the judgment.

The actor is *court*, the action is *modify*, and the object of the action is *judgment*. What is the purpose of the first four words in the sentence? None. Not only are they wasted words, but they preempt the most important position in the sentence — the beginning, where the reader wants to find the actor and the action.

When rewritten, the sentence is both shorter and stronger than the original:

The court can modify the judgment.

Be alert when you find a sentence or clause that begins with *it* or *there*, followed by a form of the verb *to be*. Does the *it* or *there* refer to something specific? If not, you may be wasting words. Consider this passage:

The summons arrived this morning. It is on your desk.

The second sentence begins with *it*, followed by a form of the verb *to be*. The sentence is not faulty, however, because the *it* obviously refers back to *summons* in the prior sentence. But what does the *it* refer to in the following sentence?

> It is obvious that the summons was not properly served.

The *it* does not refer to anything specific; rather, it points off into the fog somewhere. The sentence should be revised to read:

> Obviously the summons was not properly served.

Here is a final example:

> There were no reasons offered by the court for denying punitive damages.

Note that *there* is followed by *were*, a form of the verb *to be*. The *there* points off into the fog. The actor in the sentence is *court*, but it is hidden away in the middle of the sentence. The sentence would be shorter and stronger if it read:

> The court offered no reasons for denying punitive damages.

Exercise 4

Rewrite these sentences, omitting surplus words and focusing on the actor, the action, and the object of the action.

1. There are three misstatements of fact in appellant's opening brief.
2. It is not necessary for the witness to sign the deposition transcript until the errors are corrected.
3. In approving a class action settlement, it is imperative for the court to guard the interests of class members who are not present.

4. There is nothing to tell us whether this misconduct on the part of trial counsel influenced the jury's verdict.

5. It has been nine weeks since we served our first set of interrogatories.

Answers on page 80. More exercises on page 92.

Do Not Use Redundant Legal Phrases

Why do lawyers use the term *null and void*? According to the dictionary, either *null* or *void* by itself would do the job. But the lawyer's pen seems impelled to write *null and void*, as though driven by primordial instinct. An occasional lawyer, perhaps believing that *null and void* looks naked by itself, will write *totally null and void*, or perhaps *totally null and void and of no further force or effect whatsoever*.

Null and void is a lawyer's tautology — a needless string of words with the same or nearly the same meaning. Here are other common examples:

alter or change

cease and desist

confessed and
  acknowledged

convey, transfer,
  and set over

for and during the
  period

force and effect

last will and
  testament

made and entered
  into

order and direct

perform and
  discharge

rest, residue, and
  remainder

save and except

for and during the period	rest, residue, and remainder
force and effect	save and except
free and clear	suffer or permit
full and complete	true and correct
give, devise and bequeath	undertake and agree
good and sufficient	unless and until

Lawyer's tautologies have ancient roots. Professor Mellinkoff explains[10] that, at several points in history, the English and their lawyers had two languages to choose from: first, a choice between the language of the Celts and that of their Anglo-Saxon conquerors; later, a choice between English and Latin; and later still, a choice between English and French. Lawyers started using a word from each language, joined in a pair, to express a single meaning. (For example, *free and clear* comes from the Old English *freo* and the Old French *cler*.) This redundant doubling was sometimes used for clarity, sometimes for emphasis, and sometimes just because it was the fashion. Doubling became traditional in legal language, and it persisted long after any practical purpose was dead.

Ask a modern lawyer why he or she uses a term like *suffer or permit* in a simple apartment lease. The first answer will likely be: "for precision." True, *suffer* has a slightly different meaning than its companion *permit*. But *suffer* in this sense is now rare in ordinary usage, and *permit* would do the job if it were used alone.

The lawyer might then tell you that *suffer or permit* is better because it is a traditional legal term of art. Traditional it may be, but a term of art it is not. A term of art is a short expression that (a) conveys a fairly well-agreed meaning, and (b) saves the many words that would otherwise be needed to convey that meaning. *Suffer or permit* fails to satisfy the second condition, and perhaps the first as well.

The word *hearsay* is an example of a true term of art. First, its core meaning is fairly well agreed in modern evidence law, although its meaning at the margin has always inspired scholarly debate.[11] Second, *hearsay* enables a lawyer to use one word instead of many to say that a statement is being offered into evidence to prove that what it asserts is true, and that the statement is not one made by the declarant while testifying at the trial or hearing. Any word that can say all that deserves our praise and deference. But *suffer or permit* does not.

Suffer or permit probably found its way into that apartment lease because the lawyer was working from a form that had been used around the office for years. The author of the form, perhaps long dead, probably worked from some even older form that might, in turn, have been inspired by a formbook or some now defunct appellate case where the phrase was used but not examined.

If you want your writing to have a musty, formbook smell, by all means use as many tautological phrases as you can find. If you want it to be crisp, do not use any. When one looms up on your page, stop to see if one of the several words, or perhaps a fresh word, will carry your intended meaning. You will find, for example, that the phrase *last will and testament* can be replaced by the single word *will*.

This is not as simple as it sounds. Lawyers are busy, cautious people, and they cannot afford to make mistakes. The old, redundant phrase has worked in the past; a new one may somehow raise a question. To check it in the law library will take time, and time is the lawyer's most precious commodity. But remember — once you slay one of these old monsters, it will stay dead for the rest of your legal career. If your memory is short, keep a card file of slain redundancies. Such trophies distinguish a lawyer from a scrivener.

Exercise 5

In the following passage you will find all the kinds of surplus words discussed in Chapter Two. Rewrite the passage, omitting as many surplus words as you can.

~~We turn now to~~ Turning to the request which ~~has been made by~~ the plaintiff ~~for~~ made the issuance of injunctive relief. ~~With respect to this request,~~ the argument has been made by the defendant that injunctive relief is not necessary because ~~of the fact that~~ the exclusionary clause is already ~~null and~~ void ~~by reason of~~ the prior order ~~and decree~~ of this court. ~~This being the case,~~ therefore the exclusionary clause can have no further ~~force or~~ effect, and the defendant argues that ~~in such an instance~~ full and complete relief can be given without the issuance of an injunction. ~~There is~~ obvious merit in defendant's contention, ~~and it is for that reason that~~ therefore we have reached a decision not to grant injunctive relief ~~herein.~~

Answer on page 80. More exercises on page 93.

CHAPTER THREE

Use Base Verbs, Not Nominalizations

A t its core, the law is not abstract. It is part of a real world full of people who live and move and do things to other people. Car drivers *collide*. Plaintiffs *complain*. Judges *decide*. Defendants *pay*.

To express this life and motion, a writer must use verbs — action words. The purest verb form is the base verb, like *collide, complain, decide,* and *pay*. Base verbs are simple creatures. They cannot tolerate adornment. If you try to dress them up, you squash their life and motion. The base verb *collide* can be decked out as a noun, *collision*. Likewise, *complain* becomes *complaint*. *Decide* becomes *decision*. *Pay* becomes *payment*.

A base verb that has been turned into a noun is called a "nominalization." Lawyers and bureaucrats love nominalizations. Lawyers and bureaucrats do not *act* — they *take actions*. They do not *assume* — they *make assumptions*. They do not *conclude* — they *draw conclusions*.

If you use nominalizations instead of base verbs, surplus words begin to swarm like gnats. "Please *state* why you *object* to the question," comes out like this: "Please *make a statement* of why you *are interposing an objection* to the question." The base verb *state* can do the work all alone. But to get the same work out of *statement*, you need a supporting verb (*make*), an article (*a*), and a preposition (*of*). The word *objection* attracts a similar cloud of surplus words.

You can spot most of the common nominalizations by their endings:

al	ment	ant
ence	ion	ent
ancy	ency	ance
ity		

Not all words with those endings are nominalizations. Further, not all nominalizations are bad; sometimes you cannot avoid them. But do not overuse them — when you find one on your page, stop to see if you can make your sentence shorter and stronger by using a base verb instead.

Exercise 6

Rewrite these sentences omitting surplus words and using base verbs in place of nominalizations.

1. Section 1038 has pertinence to any contract that makes provision for attorney fees.

2. Commencement of discovery is not dependent on the judge's consideration of the motion.

3. We are in agreement with your position, but if it is your intention to cause delay, we will stand in opposition to you.

4. The effectuation of improvement in downstream

water quality has as a requirement our termination of the pollution of the headwaters.

5. If there is a continuation of this breach, my client will effect an immediate termination of the contract.

6. Amendment of the interrogatory answer is clearly proper, but if we make an amendment at this point in time, the court may have some suspicion with respect to our client's good faith.

7. Fulfillment of the testator's wishes is an impossibility unless this court orders an invalidation of the *inter vivos* transfer.

8. Cooperation with you is our sincere desire, and we hope you are willing to undertake serious reconsideration of your position. Your refusal to do so, and your failure to accomplish the completion of the work on schedule, would cause us to commence impoundment of your funds.

Answers on page 81. More exercises on page 94.

CHAPTER FOUR

Prefer the Active Voice

When you use a verb in the active voice, the subject of the sentence acts: "The union *filed* a complaint." (The subject is *union*, and the active verb is *filed*.) When you use a verb in the passive voice, the subject of the sentence is acted upon: "A complaint *was filed* by the union." (Now the subject is *complaint*, and the passive verb is *was filed*.)

The passive voice has two disadvantages. First, it takes more words. When you say, "The union filed a complaint," *filed* does the work by itself. But when you say, "A complaint was filed by the union," the verb *filed* requires a supporting verb (*was*) and a preposition (*by*). Here are other examples:

Passive	Active
the ruling was made by the trial judge	the trial judge ruled
our interpretation is supported by the legislative history	the legislative history supports our interpretation
the trust was intended by the trustor to	the trustor intended the trust to

The second disadvantage of the passive voice is its potential for ambiguity. With the active voice, you can usually tell who is doing what to whom. With the passive voice, however, the writer can omit the identity of the actor. That kind of construction is called a "truncated passive." For example:

John kicked the ball.	*active voice*
The ball was kicked by John.	*passive voice*
The ball was kicked.	*truncated passive*
A kicking action was accomplished.	*truncated passive & nominalization*

Bureaucrats like the truncated passive because it cloaks the actor in fog — the reader cannot discover what flesh-and-blood person is responsible for the action. For example: "It has been determined that you do not qualify for benefits under this program." Who determined it? The reader is left to wonder.

The truncated passive can be especially troublesome in legal writing. Consider this patent license provision:

> All improvements of the patented invention which are made hereafter shall promptly be disclosed, and failure to do so shall be deemed a material breach of this license agreement.

Who must disclose improvements to whom? Must the licensee disclose improvements it makes to the licensor?

Must the licensor disclose improvements it makes to the licensee? Must each party disclose the improvements it makes to the other party? If it ever becomes important, the parties will probably have to fight it out in an expensive lawsuit.

The passive voice does have its proper uses. First, you can use it when the thing done is important, and the one who did it is not:

> The subpoena was served on January 19th.

Second, you can use it when the actor is unknown:

> The ledgers were mysteriously destroyed.

Third, you can use it to place a strong element at the end of the sentence for emphasis:

> When he walked through the door, he was shot.

Fourth, you can use it on those rare occasions when detached abstraction is appropriate:

> All humans were created equal in the eyes of the law.

But elsewhere, use the active voice; it will make your writing stronger and clearer.

Exercise 7

Rewrite these sentences, omitting surplus words and using the active voice. Supply any missing information that you need.

1. Clients' funds which have been received by an attorney must be put into the Client Trust Account.

2. This agreement may be terminated by either party by thirty days' notice being given to the other party.

3. Each month price lists were exchanged between the defendant manufacturers, and it was agreed by them that all sales would be made at list prices or above.

4. If I am not survived by my husband by thirty days, my children are to receive such of those items of my personal property as may be selected for them by my executor.

5. It was insisted by the supplier that the goods were of merchantable quality.

6. In certain instances, a Form 242A request must be received and approved before customs clearance will be granted. No action will be taken with respect to customs clearance until the Form 242A request has been acted upon favorably. Where it is determined that no Form 242A request need be filed, steps may be taken to effect customs clearance without delay.

Answers on page 81. More exercises on page 95.

CHAPTER FIVE

Use Short Sentences

For several hundred years, English-speaking lawyers have been addicted to long, complicated sentences. The long sentence habit began before English had a regular system of punctuation. But in law, the habit persisted long after orderly division of thought had become routine in ordinary English prose. When lawyers write, they deliver to the reader in one gigantic package all their main themes, supporting reasons, details, qualifications, exceptions, and conclusions. In particular, statutes and regulations wind on line after line, perhaps on the theory that if the readers come to a period they will rush out to violate the law without bothering to read on to the end. Consider this criminal statute:

> Any person who, by means of any machine, instrument, or contrivance, or in any manner, intentionally taps, or makes any unauthorized connection, whether physically, electrically, acoustically, inductively, or otherwise, with any telegraph or telephone wire, line, cable, or instrument of any internal telephonic communications system, or who willfully and without consent of all parties to the communication, or in an unauthorized manner, reads, or attempts to read, or to learn the contents or meaning of any message, report, or communication while the same is in transit or passing over any such wire, line or cable, or is being sent from or received at any place within this state; or who uses, or attempts to use, in any manner, or

for any purpose, or to communicate in any way, any information so obtained, or who aids, agrees with, employs, or conspires with any person or persons to unlawfully do, or permit, or cause to be done any of the acts or things mentioned above in this section, is punishable by a fine not exceeding two thousand five hundred dollars ($2,500), or by imprisonment in the county jail not exceeding one year, or by imprisonment in the state prison not exceeding three years, or by both such fine and imprisonment in the county jail or in the state prison.[12]

That sentence contains 242 words and no fewer than eighteen separate thoughts. No wonder it is hard to swallow.

Pity the Reader

Long sentences make legal writing hard to understand. To prove this to yourself, read the following passage at your normal speed. Then ask yourself what it means.

In a trial by jury, the court may, when the convenience of witnesses or the ends of justice would be promoted thereby, on motion of a party, after notice and hearing, make an order, no later than the close of the pretrial conference in cases in which such pretrial conference is to be held, or in other cases, no later than 10 days before the trial date, that the trial of the issue of liability shall precede the trial of any other issue in the case.

The subject matter of that passage is not profound or complicated, but the passage is hard to understand. It consists of a single sentence, eighty-six words long, containing five pieces of information:

1. In a jury case, the liability issue may be tried before any other issue.

2. The judge may order the liability issue to be tried first if that will serve the convenience of witnesses or the ends of justice.

3. The judge may make the order on a party's motion, after notice and hearing.

4. In a case with a pretrial conference, the judge may make the order no later than the end of the conference.

5. In a case with no pretrial conference, the judge may make the order no later than ten days before the trial date.

The original passage is hard to understand for two reasons. First, the single-sentence format caused the author to distort the logical order of the five pieces of information. The first thing the readers want to know is what the passage is about. It is about the trial of the liability issue before other issues. But before the readers discover that, they must climb through a thicket of subsidiary ideas and arrive at the last twenty words of the sentence.

Second, the single-sentence format strains the reader's memory. The subject of the sentence (*court*) appears at word seven. At word thirty-two, the verb (*make*) finally shows up. Part of the object (*an order*) comes next, but the critical part remains hidden until the reader arrives, breathless, at word sixty-eight. By then the reader has forgotten the subject and verb and must search back in the sentence to find them.

The remedy for such a passage is simple. Instead of one long sentence containing five thoughts, use five sentences, each containing one thought. Here is one way the passage could be rewritten:

In a jury case, the court may order the liability issue to
be tried before any other issue. The court may make such
an order if doing so serves the convenience of witnesses
or the ends of justice. The court may make the order on
a party's motion, after notice and hearing. In a case with
a pretrial conference, the court may make the order no
later than the end of the conference. In a case with no
pretrial conference, the court may make the order no later
than ten days before the trial date.

Instead of one eighty-seven word sentence, we now have
five sentences with an average length of eighteen words.
Each sentence contains only one main thought, and the
thoughts follow in logical sequence.

Use Short Sentences

Passages like the one above suggest a two-part guide
to clarity and ease of understanding in legal writing:

1. In *most* sentences, put only one main thought.
2. Keep the *average* sentence length below
   twenty-five words.[13]

Do not misinterpret this guide. Part 1 says that *most*
sentences should contain only one main thought — it
does *not* say that *every* sentence should contain only one
main thought. Part 2 says that the *average* length of your
sentences should be less than twenty-five words — it
does *not* say that *every* sentence should be twenty-five
words or less. A succession of short, simple sentences
sounds choppy:

Defense counsel objected to the question. She argued that

it called for hearsay. The court overruled the objection. The witness was allowed to answer.

You need an occasional longer sentence in which two or more closely related thoughts are joined:

> Defense counsel objected to the question, arguing that it called for hearsay; the court overruled the objection, and the witness was allowed to answer.

When you write a long sentence, however, bear in mind Mark Twain's advice. After recommending short sentences as the general rule, he added:

> At times [the writer] may indulge himself with a long one, but he will make sure there are no folds in it, no vaguenesses, no parenthetical interruptions of its view as a whole; when he has done with it, it won't be a sea-serpent with half of its arches under the water; it will be a torch-light procession.[14]

Exercise 8

Rewrite these passages using short sentences and omitting as many surplus words as you can.

1. By establishing a technique whereby the claims of many individuals can be resolved at the same time, class actions serve an important function in our judicial system in eliminating the possibility of repetitious litigation and providing claimants with a method of obtaining enforcement of claims which

would otherwise be too small to warrant individual litigation.

2. While there are instances in which consumer abuse and exploitation result from advertising which is false, misleading, or irrelevant, it does not necessarily follow that these cases need to be remedied by governmental intervention in the marketplace because it is possible for consumers' interests to be protected through resort to the courts, either by consumers themselves or by those competing sellers who see their market shares decline in the face of inroads based on such advertising.

3. Absent from the majority opinion is any consideration of the fact that the individual states, both as a matter of common law and additionally as a matter of federal constitutional law, have traditionally been regarded as sovereigns, in consequence of which legal doctrines such as laches, acquiescence, estoppel, as well as statutes of limitations of the type at issue in the present litigation, are not generally applied to claims made by states.

Answers on page 82. More exercises on page 96.

CHAPTER SIX

Arrange Your Words with Care

Avoid Wide Gaps Between the Subject, the Verb, and the Object

To make your writing easy to understand, most[15] of your sentences should follow the normal English word order — first the subject, next the verb, and then the object (if there is one):

subject   verb

The defendant demurred.

subject   verb   object

The defendant filed six affidavits.

In seeking to understand a sentence, the reader's mind searches for the subject, the verb, and the object. If those three key elements are set out in that order and close together in the sentence, then the reader will understand quickly.

Lawyers, however, like to test the agility of their readers by making them leap wide gaps between the subject and the verb and between the verb and the object. For example:

A claim, which in the case of negligent misconduct shall not exceed $500, and in the case of intentional miscon-

duct shall not exceed $1,000, may be filed with the Office
of the Administrator by any injured party.

In that sentence, the reader must leap a twenty-two word
gap to get from the subject (*claim*) to the verb (*may be
filed*). The best remedy for a gap that wide is to turn the
intervening words into a separate sentence:

Any injured party may file a claim with the Office of the
Administrator. A claim shall not exceed $500 for negli-
gent misconduct, nor $1,000 for intentional misconduct.

Smaller gaps between subject and verb can be
closed by moving the intervening words to the beginning or the end of the sentence:

Gap	Gap Closed
This agreement, unless revocation has occurred at an earlier date, shall expire on November 1, 1992.	Unless sooner revoked, this agreement shall expire on November 1, 1992.
The defendant, in addition to having to pay punitive damages, may be liable for plaintiff's costs and attorney fees.	The defendant may have to pay plaintiff's costs and attorney fees, in addition to punitive damages.

The problem is the same when the gap comes between
the verb and the object:

The proposed statute gives to any person who suffers financial injury by reason of discrimination based on race,

religion, sex, or physical handicap a cause of action for treble damages.

Here a twenty-one word gap comes between the verb (*gives*) and the direct object (*cause of action*). One remedy is to make two sentences. Another is to move the intervening words to the end of the sentence:

> The proposed statute gives a cause of action for treble damages to any person who suffers financial injury because of discrimination based on race, religion, sex, or physical handicap.

Exercise 9

Close the gaps in each sentence by moving the intervening words or by splitting the sentence into two. When you rewrite, omit surplus words.

1. A response must, within twenty days after service of the petition has been made, be filed with the hearing officer.

2. The attorney-client privilege, while applying to the client's revelation of a past crime, has no application when the client seeks the aid of the attorney with respect to the planning or carrying out of a future crime.

3. The sole eyewitness, having seen the accident from the window of an apartment which was on the seventh floor of a building located one-half block in a northerly direction from the intersection, tes-

tified that she did not see which car made the first entry into the intersection.

4. Jose Cruz, who was the plaintiff's grandfather, later transferred, by a deed of gift which was bitterly contested by the heirs but which was ultimately upheld by the probate court, the 200 acres that are now in dispute.

Answers on page 83. More exercises on page 97.

Avoid Nested Modifiers

When I was a child, one of my favorite toys was a figure carved from smooth dark wood, the figure of a seated, round Navajo woman. She came apart in the middle to reveal an identical but smaller woman inside. The second woman likewise came apart to reveal a third, and the third a fourth.

Perverse lawyers write sentences that are constructed like my Navajo women. For example:

> Defendant, who was driving a flatbed truck that was laden with a tangle of old furniture some of which was not tied down securely, stopped without warning.

Here is the same sentence written with brackets and parentheses:

> Defendant {who was driving a flatbed truck [that was laden with a tangle of old furniture (some of which was not tied down securely)]} stopped without warning.

That sentence is like my Navajo women because it contains a set of modifying phrases, each nested inside the next. The sentence is hard to understand because the reader must mentally supply brackets and parentheses to keep the modifiers straight.

The best remedy for such a sentence is to take apart the nest of modifiers and put some of the information in a separate sentence. Consider this passage for example:

> A claim for exemption, which in the case of a dwelling that is used for housing not more than a single family shall not exceed $30,000 or the fair market value, whichever is less, may be filed with the Administrator within 90 days after receipt of notice.

When broken in two, the passage reads like this:

> A claim for exemption may be filed with the Administrator within 90 days after receipt of notice. The claim for a single family dwelling cannot exceed $30,000, or the fair market value, whichever is less.

Exercise 10

Rewrite these sentences without the nested modifiers. As you rewrite, omit surplus words.

1. Appellant, which was represented in this case by the firm of Bishop & Donald, counsel of long experience in government contract litigation, a field that requires no small degree of expertise, must have recognized the weakness of its claim.

2. The Model Rules of Professional Conduct require an attorney to place all funds received on behalf of a client, excluding advances for attorney fees not yet earned, as to which the potential for misuse

nevertheless seems clear, in the attorney's client trust fund account.

Answers on page 83. More exercises on page 98.

When Necessary, Tabulate

Sometimes the shortest, clearest way to present a complicated piece of material is in one long sentence, split up like a laundry list. This device is called "tabulation." Here is a sentence that could benefit from tabulation:

You can qualify for benefits under Section 43 if you are sixty-four or older and unable to work, and that section also provides benefits in the event that you are blind in one eye, or both eyes, or are permanently disabled in the course of your employment.

When tabulated, the sentence looks like this:

You can qualify for benefits under Section 43 if you meet any one of the following conditions:

- You are 64 or older and are unable to work; *or*
- You are blind in one or both eyes; *or*
- You are permanently disabled in the course of your employment.

When you tabulate, follow these conventions:

1. Each item in the list must be of the same class. Don't make a list like this:

a. bread;
b. eggs;
c. Czar Nicholas II.

2. Each item in the list must fit, in substance and grammar, with the material in front of the colon and the material following the list. Don't make a list like this:

    a. jurisdiction;

    b. venue;

    c. preparing charts for Dr. Sullivan's testimony.

3. After each item in the list, except the last, put a semicolon followed by *or* (if the list is disjunctive) or *and* (if the list is conjunctive). If both the list and the items are short, and if the reader will not become confused, you can omit the *and* or *or* after all except the next-to-last item.

As shown above, tabulation can also be used to bring order to a series of related, complete sentences.

Exercise 11

Use tabulation to clarify this passage.

Venue would be proper, unless the claim is framed as a federal question, in the Southern District of New York, if that is where the plaintiff resides, or in the Eastern District of California, assuming that the defendant does business in that judicial district, or in the Northern District of Illinois, if that turns out to be the place where the events in question happened.

Answer on page 84. More exercises on page 99.

Put Modifying Words Close to What They Modify

In some languages, the order of words within a sentence does not affect the meaning of the sentence. But in English, word order does affect meaning, as this sentence shows:

> The defendant was arrested for fornicating under a little-used state statute.

Modifying words tend to do their work on whatever you put them near. Therefore, as a general rule, put modifying words as close as you can to the words you want them to modify. That will help avoid sentences like these:

> My client has discussed your proposal to fill the drainage ditch with his partners.

> Being beyond any doubt insane, Judge Weldon ordered the petitioner's transfer to a state mental hospital.

Beware of the "squinting" modifier — one that sits mid-sentence and can be read to modify either what precedes it or what follows it:

> A trustee who steals dividends often cannot be punished.

What does *often* modify? Does the sentence tell us that crime frequently pays? Or that frequent crime pays?

Once discovered, a squinting modifier is easy to cure. Either choose a word that does not squint, or rearrange the sentence to avoid the ambiguity. For example:

> When workers are injured frequently no compensation is paid.

If that means that injured workers often receive no compensation, the squinting modifier could be moved to the front of the sentence, like this:

> Frequently, workers who are injured receive no compensation.

The word *only* is a notorious troublemaker. For example, in the following sentence the word *only* could go in any of seven places and produce a half a dozen different meanings:

> She said that he shot her.

To keep *only* under control, put it immediately before the word you want it to modify. If it creates ambiguity in that position, try to isolate it at the beginning or ending of the sentence:

Ambiguous	Clear
Lessee shall use the vessel only for recreation.	Lessee shall use the vessel for recreation only.
Shares are sold to the public only by the parent corporation	Only the parent corporation sells shares to the public.

Watch out for ambiguity in sentences like this one:

> The grantor was Maxwell Aaron, the father of Sarah Aaron, who later married Pat Snyder.

Who married Pat — Maxwell or Sarah? Some lawyers try to clear up this kind of ambiguity by piling on more words:

The grantor was Maxwell Aaron, father of Sarah Aaron, which said Maxwell Aaron later married Pat Snyder.

But it's easier than that. You can usually avoid ambiguity by placing the relative pronoun (like *who*, *which*, and *that*) right after the word to which it relates. If Pat's spouse were Maxwell, the sentence could be rearranged to read:

The grantor was Sarah Aaron's father, Maxwell Aaron, who later married Pat Snyder.

Sometimes a relative pronoun will not behave, no matter where you put it:

Claims for expenses, which must not exceed $100, must be made within 30 days.

What must not exceed $100 — the claims or the expenses? Here the best remedy is simply to omit the relative pronoun:

Claims for expenses must not exceed $100 and must be made within 30 days.

or

Expenses must not exceed $100. Claims for expenses must be made within 30 days.

Exercise 12

Rewrite these sentences to solve the modifier problems. If a sentence has more than one possible meaning, select whichever one you wish and rewrite the sentence to express that meaning unambiguously.

1. The plaintiff's pain can be alleviated only by expensive therapy.

2. Being ignorant of the law, the attorney argued that his client should receive a light sentence.

3. Defendant's argument overlooks an amendment to the statute which was enacted in 1984.

4. Under Section 309, attorney fees only can be awarded when the claim is brought without good faith.

5. Apparently this special tax provision was intended to encourage the production of cotton in the eyes of Congress.

Answers on page 84. More exercises on page 100.

CHAPTER SEVEN

Use Familiar, Concrete Words

H ere are two ways a lawyer might begin a letter to a client to explain why the lawyer's bill is higher than the client expected:

Example One

> The statement for professional services which you will find enclosed herewith is, in all likelihood, somewhat in excess of your expectations. In the circumstances, I believe it is incumbent upon me to avail myself of this opportunity to provide you with an explanation of the causes therefor. It is my considered judgment that three factors are responsible for this development. . . .

Example Two

> The bill I am sending you with this letter is probably higher than you expected, and I would like to explain the three reasons why. . . .

Example One is awful, is it not? It contains many of the faults we have already discussed — too many nominalizations, for example. But notice also the choice of words in Example One. Why does its author say *statement for professional services* instead of *bill*? The client calls it a bill. So does the lawyer, usually. By tradition, the bill itself can be captioned *statement for professional services*. But this is supposed to be a friendly, candid letter to a client; let us call a bill *a bill.*

Why does the author of Example One use *herewith* and *therefor?* To give the letter the stink of old law books? Why does the author use airy, abstract words like *circumstances, factors,* and *development?* Do they somehow add dignity? Finally, why does the author use ponderous phrases instead of the simple words used in Example Two?

Example One	**Example Two**
in all likelihood	probably
in excess of your expectations	higher than you expected
explanation of the causes	explain why

Use Concrete Words

To grip and move your reader's mind, use concrete words, not abstractions. For example, here is how Exodus 8:7 describes one of Moses's plagues on Egypt:

> He lifted up the rod and smote the waters of the river . . . and all the waters that were in the river were turned to blood. And the fish that were in the river died; and the river stank, and the Egyptians could not drink the water of the river; and there was blood throughout all the land of Egypt.

Now suppose that same event were described in the language of a modern environmental impact report:

> The water was impacted by his rod, whereupon a pol-
> luting effect was achieved. The consequent toxification
> reduced the conditions necessary for the sustenance of
> the indigenous population of aquatic vertebrates below
> the level of viability. Olfactory discomfort standards were
> substantially exceeded, and potability declined. Social,
> economic, and political disorientation were experienced
> to an unprecedented degree.

The lure of abstract words is strong for lawyers. Lawyers want to be cautious and to cover every possibility, while leaving room to wiggle out if necessary. The vagueness of abstract words therefore seems attractive. Particularly attractive are words like *basis, situation, consideration, facet, character, factor, degree, aspect,* and *circumstances:*

> In our present circumstances, the budgetary aspect is a
> factor which must be taken into consideration to a greater
> degree.

Perhaps that means "now we must think more about money," but the meaning is a shadow in the fog of abstract words.

Do not mistake abstraction of that sort for the intentional, artful vagueness sometimes required in legal writing. For example, judicial opinions sometimes use an intentionally vague phrase to provide a general compass heading when it is not possible to map the trail in detail. In *Bates v. State Bar of Arizona,*[16] the Supreme Court announced that lawyer advertising is protected by the free speech clause of the first amendment. The Court wanted to tell the states that they could regulate lawyer advertising some, but not too much. The Court could not then tell how much would be too much, so it said that states may impose *"reasonable restrictions"* on the time, place and manner of lawyer advertising. The phrase is intentionally vague. It gives general guidance, but it postpones specific guidance until specific facts come before the Court in later cases.

Intentional vagueness is likewise used in drafting statutes, contracts, and the like, when the drafter cannot foresee every specific set of facts that may arise. But vagueness is a virtue only if it is both necessary and intentional. Knowing when to be vague and when to press for more concrete terms is part of the art of lawyering.

Use Familiar Words

Aristotle put the case for familiar words this way: "Style to be good must be clear. . . . Speech which fails to convey a plain meaning will fail to do just what speech has to do. . . . Clearness is secured by using the words . . . that are current and ordinary."[17] Given a choice between a familiar word and one that will send your reader groping for the dictionary, use the familiar word. The reader's attention is a precious commodity, and you cannot afford to waste it by creating distractions.

Unlike many writers, attorneys usually know who their readers will be, and their choice of words can be tailored accordingly. A patent lawyer who is writing a brief to be filed in the United States Court of Appeals for the Federal Circuit can use legal terms that might be perplexing if used in a letter to the lawyer's inventor-client. Conversely, in writing to the inventor-client, the patent lawyer can use scientific terms that would be hypertechnical if used in a legal brief. In either case, the convenience of the reader must take precedence over the self-gratification of the writer.

Even among familiar words, prefer the simple to the stuffy. Don't say *termination* if *end* will do as well. Don't use *expedite* for *hurry*, or *elucidate* for *explain*, or *utilize* for *use*. Do not conclude that your vocabulary should shrink to preschool size. If an unfamiliar word is fresh and fits your need better than any other, use it — but don't *utilize* it.

Do Not Use Lawyerisms

Lawyerisms are words like *aforementioned, whereas, res gestae,* and *hereinafter.* They give writing a legal smell, but they carry little or no legal substance. When they are used in writing addressed to nonlawyers, they baffle and annoy. When used in other legal writing, they give a false sense of precision and sometimes obscure a dangerous gap in analysis.

A lawyer's words should not differ without reason from the words used in ordinary English. Sometimes there is a reason. For example, the Latin phrase *res ipsa loquitur* has become a term of art[18] that lawyers use to communicate among themselves, conveniently and with a fair degree of precision, about a tort law doctrine.[19] But too often lawyers use Latin or archaic English phrases needlessly. Sometimes they do it out of habit or haste —the old phrase is the one they learned in law school, and they have never taken time to question its use. Other times they do it believing mistakenly that the old phrase's meaning cannot be expressed in ordinary English, or that the old phrase is somehow more precise than ordinary English.

Consider, for example, the word *said* in its archaic use as an adjective. No lawyer in dinner table conversation says: "The green beans are excellent; please pass said green beans." Yet legal pleadings come out like this:

> The object of said conspiracy among said defendants was to fix said retail prices of said products in interstate commerce.

Lawyers who use *said* claim that it is more precise than ordinary words like *the*, or *this*, or *those*. They say it means "the exact same one mentioned above." But the extra precision is either illusory or unnecessary, as the above example shows. If only one conspiracy has been mentioned in the preceding material, we will not mistake *this* conspiracy for some other conspiracy, and *said* is unnecessary. If more than one conspiracy has been previously mentioned, *said* does not tell us which of the several is meant. The extra precision is thus illusory. If *the* were put in place of all the *saids*, the sentence would be no less precise and much less clumsy.

Aforementioned is *said's* big brother, and it is just as useless. "The fifty-acre plot aforementioned shall be divided. . . ." If only one fifty-acre plot has been mentioned before, then *aforementioned* is unnecessary, and if more than one fifty-acre plot has been mentioned before, then *aforementioned* is imprecise. When precision is important, use a specific reference: "The fifty-acre plot described in paragraph 2(f) shall be divided. . . ."

Res gestae is an example of a Latin lawyerism that can obscure a dangerous gap in analysis. Translated, it means "things done." In the early 1800's, it was used to denote statements that were made as part of the transaction in issue (the "things done") and that were therefore admissible in evidence despite the hearsay rule.

Perhaps because *res gestae* is far removed from ordinary English, lawyers and judges began to treat it as a ragbag. They used it carelessly to cover many different kinds of statements made at or about the time of the transaction in issue.[20] With policy and analysis obscured, *res gestae* became little more than a label to express the conclusion that a particular statement ought to be admitted into evidence over hearsay objection. Wigmore said: "The phrase 'res gestae' has long been not only entirely useless, but even positively harmful. . . . It is harmful, because by its ambiguity it invites the confusion of one rule with another and thus creates uncertainty as to the limitations of both."[21]

The moral is this: Do not be too impressed by the Latin and archaic English words you read in law books. Their antiquity does not make them superior. When your pen is poised to write a lawyerism, stop to see if your meaning can be expressed as well or better in a word or two of ordinary English.

Exercise 13

Rewrite these sentences using familiar, concrete words and omitting surplus words.

1. Said defendant International Business Machines Corporation is hereinafter referred to as "IBM".
2. The prisoner's aptitude for acclimatization to lack of confinement is one factor which must be taken into account in the deliberations of the Parole Board.

3. The purpose of paragraph 9(f) is *in ambiguo*, but it appears to be *pro majori cautela*.

4. The effectuation of reform of penal institutions is dependent to some degree upon the extent of awareness of current events in that sector among members of the general populace.

5. The patent laws which give a seventeen-year monopoly on "making, using, or selling the invention" are *in pari materia* with the antitrust laws and modify them *pro tanto*. That was the *ratio decidendi* of the *General Electric* case.

Answers on page 85. More exercises on page 100.

Avoid Shotgunning

When we lawyers want to be precise and to cover every possibility, we too often use the shotgun approach — we take rough aim and loose a blast of words, hoping that at least one of them might hit the target. For example, here is a typical criminal statute:

> Every person who . . . overdrives, overloads, drives when overloaded, overworks, tortures, torments, deprives of necessary sustenance, drink, or shelter, cruelly beats, mutilates, or cruelly kills any animal, or causes or procures any animal to be so overdriven, overloaded, overworked, tortured, tormented, deprived of necessary sustenance, drink or shelter, or to be cruelly beaten, mutilated, or cruelly killed . . . is guilty of a misdemeanor.[22]

The simplest remedy for shotgunning is to use a dictionary and a thesaurus to find a single word that will adequately express the intended meaning.[23] In the statute above, the single verb *"abuse"* could replace the ten-verb shotgun blast.

Sometimes the simple remedy will not suffice. For instance, the author of the animal abuse statute may have feared that a judge would find the single verb *"abuse"* too vague to give the public fair notice of the kinds of conduct covered by the statute. Where vagueness poses a real problem (as it can in criminal statutes), the best course is to choose a serviceable term and define it for the reader.[24] Then, use the term consistently throughout the document, being cautious not to depart from its defined meaning.[25]

Exercise 14

When you rewrite these passages, pay special attention to your choice of words.

1. All advance payments of rentals made hereunder shall be binding on any direct or indirect assignee, grantee, devisee, administrator, executor, heir, or successor to the lessor.

2. Tenant has not at any time heretofore made, done, committed, executed, permitted or suffered any act, deed, matter or thing whatsoever, whereby or wherewith, or by reason or means whereof the said lands and premises hereby assigned and surrendered, or any part or parcel thereof are, or is, or may, can or shall be in anywise impeached, charged, affected or incumbered.

3. It shall be and hereby is declared to be unlawful

for any person or persons to expel, discharge, or expectorate any mucus, spittle, saliva or other such substance from the mouth of said person or persons in or on or onto any public sidewalk, street, highway, boulevard, thoroughfare, building, terminal, theatre, railway train, street car, bus, trolley, ferryboat, steamer, boat, taxicab, jitney or conveyance, or in or on or onto any other public place of whatsoever kind or description, and any person or persons who do so expel, discharge, or expectorate any such substance as defined above at any place herein delineated shall be guilty of a misdemeanor.

4. At any sporting event which involves the participation of an umpire, referee, judge, director, or supervisor in connection with the conduct of such event, it is a misdemeanor for any person to offer anything of value to such umpire, referee, judge, director, or supervisor with the intent of influencing the umpiring, refereeing, judging, or supervising of such sporting event in such manner as may affect the outcome thereof.

Answers on page 86. More exercises on page 102.

CHAPTER EIGHT

Avoid Language Quirks

anguage quirks are small distractions that draw your reader's mind from *what* you are saying to *how* you are saying it. Most of what lawyers write is read by people, not because they want to, but because they have to. Their attention is therefore prone to wander. Further, they are usually surrounded by outside distractions — the ring of the telephone, the cough at the library table, and the clock that tells them time is short. Language quirks add to those distractions and thus should be avoided.

To take a simple example, most people have been told by some well-meaning teacher never to split an infinitive. An infinitive is split when a modifier is inserted between the word *to* and the verb — for example, "to never split." Even though this "rule" has been thoroughly debunked by experts,[26] it remains implanted in the subconscious caverns of some readers' minds. Those readers will be distracted when they see an infinitive split unnecessarily. Therefore, do not split an infinitive unless doing so will avoid an ambiguity or a clumsy expression. Likewise, do not end a sentence with a preposition unless you have to.

Avoid Elegant Variation

Elegant variation is practiced by writers whose

English teachers told them not to use the same word twice in one sentence. Elegant variation produces sentences like this:

> The first case was settled for $20,000, and the second piece of litigation was disposed of out of court for $30,000, while the price of the amicable accord reached in the third suit was $50,000.

The readers are left to ponder the difference between a *case*, a *piece of litigation*, and a *suit*. By the time they conclude that there is no difference, they have no patience left for *settled, disposed of out of court,* and *amicable accord,* much less for what the writer was trying to tell them in the first place.

Elegant variation is particularly vexing in technical legal writing. The reader of a legal document is entitled to assume that a shift in terms is intended to signal a shift in meaning, and the reader is justifiably puzzled at passages like this:

> The use fee shall be 1% of Franchisee's gross revenue. Franchise payment shall be made on or before the 15th day of each month.

Are *franchise payments* something different from the *use fee*? If so, what are they, and when must the *use fee* be paid?

Do not be afraid to repeat a word if it is the right word, and if repeating it will avoid confusion.

A different, but related, language quirk is the use of a word in one sense and its repetition shortly after in a different sense:

> The majority opinion gives no consideration to appellant's argument that no consideration was given for the promise.

The remedy is obvious — replace one of the pair with a different term:

> The majority opinion ignores appellant's argument that no consideration was given for the promise.

Avoid Noun Chains

A long chain of nouns used as adjectives is likely to strangle the reader. That is, noun chains create *noun chain reader strangulation problems.* Bureaucrats love noun chains. They write about *draft laboratory animal rights protection regulations* and about *public service research dissemination program proposals.* We lawyers are not immune. We have been known to file *Pretrial Doc ument Identification Request Responses.*

To bring a noun chain under control, lop off any of the descriptive words that are not essential. If that is not enough, then insert some words to break up the chain, like this: "Responses to Plaintiff's Request for Pretrial Identification of Documents."

Avoid Multiple Negatives

Beware of sentences that contain more than one negative expression. "It shall be unlawful to fail to. . . ." is an example of a double negative. The grammar is proper, but the construction is distracting — it makes the reader's mind flip from *yes* to *no* to *yes.*

In addition to ordinary negative words and prefixes (such as *not, un-,* and *non-*), many other words operate negatively (for example, *terminate, void, denial, except,*

unless, and *other than*). If you string a few of these negative words together, you can make the reader's eyes
cross, like this:

> Provided <u>however</u>, that this license shall <u>not</u> become <u>void</u>
> <u>unless</u> licensee's <u>failure</u> to provide such notice is <u>unrea-</u>
> <u>sonable</u> in the circumstances.

When you find that you have written a sentence with
multiple negatives, identify each negative term. Then
pair as many of them as you can, to turn them into pos-
itives. Finally, rewrite the sentence using as many posi-
tives and as few negatives as you can.[27] For instance, "It
shall be unlawful to fail to stop at a red light" becomes
"You must stop at a red light."

Here is a more complicated passage:

> No rate agreement shall qualify under Section 2(a) un-
> less not fewer than thirty days notice is given to all cus-
> tomers; and unless said rate agreement has been
> published, as provided above, provided however, that the
> publication requirement shall not apply to emergency
> rates; and until said rate agreement has been approved
> by the Commission.

When rewritten in the positive, the passage emerges like
this:

> To qualify under Section 2(a), a rate agreement must
> meet these three conditions:
>
> - All customers must receive at least thirty days no-
>   tice of it; and
>
> - It must be published, as provided above (but emer-
>   gency rates do not have to be published); and
>
> - It must be approved by the Commission.

Avoid Cosmic Detachment

Every legal problem involves people. Without people, there would be no legal problems. Yet legal writing too often ignores people and addresses itself to some bloodless, timeless cosmic void. For example, here is the opening substantive sentence of the new federal copyright law:

> Copyright protection subsists, in accordance with this title, in original works of authorship fixed in any tangible medium of expression, now known or later developed, from which they can be perceived, reproduced, or otherwise communicated, either directly or with the aid of a machine or device.[28]

Can you find any people in that sentence? *Authorship* is as close as you can get, and it is none too human.

When you find yourself struggling to express a complex legal idea, remember to ask yourself the key question that you learned in Chapter Two: "Who is doing what to whom?"[29] Bring those living creatures into your writing — make them move around and do things to each other. Suddenly abstraction will evaporate, and your writing will come alive.

Remember, too, that your reader is the most important person in the universe — or at least your reader thinks so. Don't be afraid to bring the readers into your sentences, and don't be afraid to call them "you." The personal form of address will help them understand how the passage relates to them.[30]

Use Strong Nouns and Verbs

Most legal writing is declaratory. It simply states the facts, without comment, and without trying to persuade anyone of anything. Statutes, apartment leases, corporate bylaws, and bills of lading fall in this category. But some legal writing does comment. Through commentary, it seeks to persuade the reader to believe what the writer believes. Legal briefs and judicial opinions are obvious examples. Where commentary is appropriate, it will be more potent if you use strong nouns and verbs, not weak nouns and verbs held afloat by adjectives and adverbs. For instance:

Adjectives and Adverbs	Nouns and Verbs
The witness intentionally testified untruthfully about the cargo.	The witness lied about the cargo.
Defendant's sales agents maliciously took advantage of people with little money and limited intelligence.	Defendant's sales agents preyed on the poor and the ignorant.

When you need to use an adjective or adverb for commentary, choose one that fits. Do not use a firey one and then douse it with water:

> rather catastrophic
> somewhat terrified
> a bit malevolently
> slightly hysterical

Similarly, do not choose a flaccid one and then try to prop it up with words like *very* and *quite*:

Weak	Strong
she was very, very angry	she was enraged
this is quite puzzling	this is baffling

Avoid Sexist Language

The very first section of the United States Code says that: "words importing the masculine gender include the feminine as well."[31] Women are tired of that, and legal writers can no longer get away with it.[32]

Whatever your personal beliefs about the role of women in society, you should avoid sexist language for the same reason that you avoid other language quirks — if you use sexist language, you will distract a part of your audience. And you will distract another part of your audience if you resort to clumsy or artificial constructions when trying to avoid sexist language.

Avoiding sexism gracefully is no easy task. Here are four suggestions that may help:

First, don't use expressions that imply value judgments based on sex. (For example, *a manly effort*, or *a member of the gentle sex.*)

Second, use sex-neutral terms where you can do so without artificiality. (For example, use *workers* instead of *workmen* and *reasonable person* instead of *reasonable man.* But don't concoct artificial terms like *waitpersons* to refer to servers in a restaurant.)

Third, use parallel construction when you are referring to both sexes. (For example, *husbands and wives*, not *men and their wives*, or *President and Mrs. Kennedy*, not *President Kennedy and Jackie*.)

Fourth, don't use sex-based pronouns when the referent may be of the opposite sex. For instance, don't use *he* every time you refer to judges. And don't use *she* either. The latter is just as distracting as the former. You can resort to the clumsy phrase *he or she* in moderation, but you can often avoid the need by using one of the following devices:

Omit the pronoun: For example, instead of *"the average citizen enjoys his time on the jury,"* you can say *"the average citizen enjoys jury duty."*

Use the second person instead of the third person: For example, instead of *"each juror must think for herself,"* you can say *"as a juror, you must think for yourself."*

Use the plural instead of the singular: For example, instead of *"each juror believes that he has done something worthwhile,"* you can say *"all jurors believe that they have done something worthwhile."*

Repeat the noun instead of using a pronoun: For example, instead of *"a juror's vote should reflect her own opinion,"* you can say *"a juror's vote should reflect that juror's own opinion."*

Alternate between masculine and feminine pronouns: For example, if you use *she* to refer to judges in one paragraph, use *he* to refer to lawyers in the next paragraph. Be aware that this device may look artificial,[33] and that if you are careless you may perform a sex change on somebody in the middle of paragraph.

Use the passive voice: For the reasons explained in Chapter Four, use this device only in desperation.

Avoid Throat-Clearing

Just as some public speakers clear their throats at every pause, some legal writers feel the need to clear the clogs from their pens every fifty words or so. The result is a collection of phrases like this:

> It is important to add that. . . .
> Clear beyond dispute is the fact that. . . .
> It may be recalled that. . . .
> It would appear to be the case that. . . .
> In this regard it is of significance that. . . .
> It is interesting to point out that. . . .

William Zinsser writes:

> If you might add, add it. If it should be pointed out, point it out. If it is interesting to note, *make* it interesting. Being told that something is interesting is the surest way of tempting the reader to find it dull. . . .[34]

Words like *clearly* are favorite throat clearers. California's former Chief Justice Roger Traynor used to tell his law clerks to strike *clearly* whenever they used it. If what is said is clear, then *clearly* is not needed, and if it is not clear, then *clearly* will not make it so.

Exercise 15

1. When you rewrite this passage, address it directly to the reader and eliminate the elegant variation:

   > The Privacy Act of 1974 requires that all governmental units inform each individual whom it asks to supply information: (1) the authority which authorizes the solicitation of the data and whether disclosure of the material is mandatory or voluntary; (2) the principal purpose or purposes for which the information is intended to be used by the agency; (3) the routine uses which may be made of the material; and (4) the effects, if any, of not providing all or part of the data requested by the unit or agency.

2. Break up these noun chains:

   (a) Law office management efficiency seminar

   (b) Attorney client trust fund bank account regulations

   (c) Cost analysis based proof burden presumptions

3. Eliminate the multiple negatives in this passage:

   > Except in cases governed by Rule 9.3, no practitioner admitted to the highest court of a sister state shall be denied admission to the bar of this court *pro hac vice*, provided, however, that admission shall be granted only upon motion duly made by a member admitted to practice in this jurisdiction.

4. The following passage is written for the occupants of a high-

rise office building, to tell them what to do in an emergency. When you rewrite it, avoid cosmic detachment:

In the event of any fire, explosion, bomb threat, storm, aircraft accident, civil disorder, or other emergency requiring evacuation from the building, whether during normal working hours or thereafter, this building is equipped with klaxon-type warning devices which will be activated. Upon hearing the warning, evacuation is to be by way of the nearest stairwell, proceeding either upward or downward, as directed by the Floor Captain.

5. Put vigor in the following passages by using appropriate nouns and verbs in place of the adjectives and adverbs:

   (a) Exposure to asbestos dust can result in very serious illness and can ultimately prove fatal.

   (b) Defendant's exceedingly negligent conduct certainly appears to have been the result of an attitude on his part that the safety of his fellow workers was not a matter of very great concern to him.

   (c) Shortly following any major industrial incident which results in numerous instances of very serious injury or cessation of life, one can be almost certain that an immediate consequence will be the descent of a large number of plantiffs' personal injury lawyers seeking to feed on the misfortune.

6. Rewrite the following passages to eliminate the sexist language:

   (a) Even the most honest witness will embellish his story unless you are in control of him at every moment of his questioning.

(b) Every trial lawyer must develop his own ways to deal with the witness who gives nonresponsive answers to his questions.

(c) Each witness must be cautioned before giving her testimony that she is to listen to the question carefully and that she is to answer only the questions that have been asked.

Answers on page 86. More exercises on page 103.

Omit Surplus Words

Avoid Compound Constructions
Avoid Word-Wasting Idioms
Focus on the Actor, the Action and the Object
Do Not Use Redundant Legal Phrases

Use Base Verbs, Not Nominalizations

Prefer the Active Voice

Use Short Sentences

Arrange Your Words With Care

Avoid Wide Gaps Between the Subject, the Verb,
 and the Object
Avoid Nested Modifiers
When Necessary, Tabulate
Put Modifying Words Close to What They Modify

Use Familiar, Concrete Words

Use Concrete Words
Use Familiar Words
Do Not Use Lawyerisms
Avoid Shotgunning

Avoid Language Quirks

Avoid Elegant Variation
Avoid Noun Chains
Avoid Multiple Negatives
Avoid Cosmic Detachment
Use Strong Nouns and Verbs
Avoid Sexist Language
Avoid Throat-Clearing

ENDNOTES

1. D. MELLINKOFF, THE LANGUAGE OF THE LAW 24 (1963).

2. Mylward v. Welden (Ch. 1596), *reprinted in* C. MONRO, ACTA CANCELLARIAE 692 (1847).

3. Letter to Joseph C. Cabell (September 9, 1817), REPRINTED IN 17 WRITINGS OF THOMAS JEFFERSON 417-18 (A. Bergh ed. 1907).

4. *See* the writings listed in Collins and Hattenhauer, *Law and Language: A Selected, Annotated Bibliography on Legal Writing*, 33 J. LEGAL EDUC. 141 (1983); Freeman, *Books on Legal Writing*, XIII SYLLABUS No. 3, p. 5 (1982).

5. Goldfarb, *Lawyer Language*, LITIGATION, Summer 1977, at 3; see also, R. GOLDFARB & J. RAYMOND, CLEAR UNDERSTANDINGS (1982).

6. *See, e.g.,* NEW YORK GEN. OBLIG. LAW §5-702 (McKinney 1984 Supp.); 26 HAWAII REV. STAT. 487 A-1 (1983 Supp.) A similar statute is now under consideration in Great Britain. California has adopted a plain English statute that requires documents written by state agencies to be "in plain, straightforward language, avoiding technical terms as much as possible, and using a coherent and easily readable style." CAL. GOVT. CODE §6215 (West 1984 Supp.)

7. *See* bibliographies cited in note 4, *supra.*

8. 248 N.Y. 339, 162 N.E. 99 (1928). I have used *Palsgraf* as an example because it is familiar to all who have studied law. In general, however, Justice Cardozo's writing style is somewhat ornate for modern tastes. If you seek good examples of modern plain English style, examine the opinions of United States Supreme Court Justice Lewis F. Powell.

9. This prescription is only part of a "Paramedic Method" devised by Professor Richard A. Lanham for rendering first aid to sick sentences. *See,* R. LANHAM, REVISING PROSE 1-8 (1979). The entire book is well worth reading.

10. D. MELLINKOFF, *supra* note 1, at 38-39, 121-22.

11. *See* FED. R. EVID. 801(c); C. MCCORMICK, EVIDENCE §§246-50 (3rd ed. 1984).

12. CAL. PEN. CODE §631(a) (West 1984 Supp.).

13. To measure sentence length, pick a representative passage and count the number of words from one period to the next. Count hyphenated words and groups of symbols as one word. Do not count citations. For example, this sentence would be counted as 20 words:

1   2   3   4   5   6   7

The twin-drive concept was obvious from IBM's

8   9   10   11   12   13

'497 patent; under the *Graham* test, 382 U.S.

14 15 16 17   18   19 20

at 17–18, that is enough to invalidate Claim 12.

When you measure a tabulated sentence (*see* pages 42–43, *supra*), regard the initial colon and the semicolons as periods. For other views about the importance of sentence length, *see generally* T. BERNSTEIN, WATCH YOUR LANGUAGE 111-21 (Antheneum paperback ed. 1976); Fry, *A Readability Formula that Saves Time*, 11 JOURNAL OF READING 513 (1968). For a more complicated readability formula, *see* R. FLESCH, HOW TO WRITE PLAIN ENGLISH: A BOOK FOR LAWYERS AND CONSUMERS 20-32 (1979).

14. As quoted in E. GOWERS, THE COMPLETE PLAIN WORDS 183 (Frazer rev. ed. 1973).

15. Occasionally you may want to invert the normal subject-verb-object order to put a strong word at the end of the sentence for emphasis. Suppose that you want to emphasize the word *perjury* in this sentence:

The stench of perjury lingers in every word the witness spoke.

By inverting the normal word order, you can put *perjury* at the end of the sentence, which is the strongest point of emphasis:

In every word the witness spoke lingers the stench of perjury.

16. 433 U.S. 350 (1977).

17. Aristotle, *Rhetoric* 1404b, in 11 THE WORKS OF ARISTOTLE (W. Ross ed. 1946).

18. *See* page 20, *supra.*

19. *See* RESTATEMENT (SECOND) OF TORTS, section 328D, comments a and b (1965).

20. *See, e.g.,* cases described in Showalter v. Western Pacific R.R., 16 Cal.2d 460, 106 P.2d 895 (1940).

21. 6 J. WIGMORE, EVIDENCE §1767 at 255 (Chadbourne rev. ed. 1976).

22. CALIF. PENAL CODE §597(b) (West 1984 Supp.)

23. R. FLESCH, HOW TO WRITE PLAIN ENGLISH: A BOOK FOR LAWYERS AND CONSUMERS 40-43 (1979).

24. By using a definition at the outset, you avoid the need to repeat the shotgun blast time and again. The definition can be either closed-ended or open-ended; each has its advantages and disadvantages. *See generally* R. DICKERSON, THE FUNDAMENTALS OF LEGAL DRAFTING 99-111 (1965).

In the animal abuse example, a closed-ended definition would state: "*abuse* means . . ." followed by a list of all the kinds of conduct that the statute is intended to cover. One advantage of a closed-ended definition is that it eliminates vagueness. One disadvantage is that the statute will not catch a villain who discovers how to abuse animals in a manner not listed in the definition. That villain's lawyer will trot out the old Latin phrase *inclusio unius est exclusio alterius* and will argue that the inclusion of some types of abuse was intended to exclude other types of abuse not mentioned.

An open-ended definition would state: "*abuse* includes but is not limited to . . ." followed by a list of examples of the kinds of conduct that the statute is intended to cover. One disadvantage of an open-ended definition is that it does not fully cure the vagueness problem. *See* D. MELLINKOFF, LEGAL WRITING: SENSE & NONSENSE 25-26 (West 1982). One advantage, however, is that the statute will catch the villain whose conduct offends the spirit, though not the letter, of the law. *See, e.g.,* California v. Clark-Van Brunt, 158 Cal. App. 3d S8, S16-S17, 205 Cal. Rptr. 144, 148-50 (L.A. Sup. App. Dept. 1984).

25. *See generally* MELLINKOFF, *supra*, 24-26, 136-138; FLESCH, *supra*, 58-69.

26. *See* T. BERNSTEIN, MISS THISTLEBOTTOM'S HOBGOBLINS 116-18 (Simon and Schuster 1971); H. FOWLER, MODERN ENGLISH USAGE 579-82 (2nd ed. E. Gowers 1965).

27. *See* R. FLESCH, HOW TO WRITE PLAIN ENGLISH: A BOOK FOR LAWYERS AND CONSUMERS 94-101 (1979); *see also* D. MELLINKOFF, LEGAL WRITING: SENSE & NONSENSE 28-38 (West 1982).

28. 17 U.S.C. §102(a) (1982).

29. *See* page 16, *supra*.

30. *See generally* C. FELSENFELD & A. SIEGEL, WRITING CONTRACTS IN PLAIN ENGLISH 114-17 (1981); FLESCH, *supra*, at 44-50.

31. 1 U.S.C. §1 (1982).

32. *See generally* Collins, *Language, History, and the Legal Process: A Profile of the "Reasonable Man,"* 8 RUT.-CAM. L.J. 311 (1977); C. MILLER & K. SWIFT, WORDS AND WOMEN (1977).

33. *See* D. MELLINKOFF, note 27, *supra*, 50. Professor Mellinkoff calls this device the "equal time doctrine" and says it is "sexist madness."

34. W. ZINSSER, ON WRITING WELL 17 (2nd ed. 1980).

Reader's Exercise Key

These are not *the* answers to the exercises. They are some of the many possible answers. You may often find that your answers are better than the ones given here. That should be cause for cheer, not puzzlement.

Exercise 1

1. Here is the original sentence with the working words underlined:

> The <u>testimony</u> that was <u>given</u> by <u>Reeves</u> <u>went</u> to the <u>heart</u> of the <u>defense</u> that <u>he</u> <u>asserted</u>, which was <u>his</u> <u>lack</u> of the <u>specific</u> <u>intent</u> to <u>escape</u>.

The original sentence could be revised to read:

> Reeves' testimony went to the heart of his defense, that he had no specific intent to escape.

With the working words underlined, the revised sentence looks like this:

> <u>Reeves'</u> <u>testimony</u> <u>went</u> to the <u>heart</u> of his <u>defense</u>, that <u>he</u> <u>had</u> <u>no</u> <u>specific</u> <u>intent</u> to <u>escape</u>.

2. Here is the original sentence with the working words underlined:

> In the event that there is a waiver of the attorney-client privilege by the client, the letters must be produced by the attorney for the purpose of inspection by the adversary party.

The original sentence could be revised to read:

> If the client waives the attorney-client privilege, the attorney must produce the letters for inspection by the adversary party.

With the working words underlined, the revised sentence looks like this:

> If the client waives the attorney-client privilege, the attorney must produce the letters for inspection by the adversary party.

Exercise 2

1. The parties were in complete agreement about the amount of rent due and about the due date.
2. For simplicity, an ordinary deed of trust would be the best.
3. Because of the *Burke* decision, the savings clause was added to avoid any ambiguity.
4. In fairness, we should not apply the new rule retroactively.

5. When the funds are received, we will transfer title, hoping to clear up all questions about this matter.

6. I cannot now recall what the letter was about.

Exercise 3

1. When the judgment is entered . . .

2. Here estoppel can be invoked . . .

3. He was sentenced to the county jail for five months . . .

4. By the terms of our contract . . .

5. No doubt the statute applies where . . .

6. The claim was clarified by a bill of particulars.

7. The trial judge must consider whether . . .

8. This offer will stand until you . . .

9. Usually the claimant's good faith is not disputed . . .

10. The plaintiff filed the complaint even though she knew that . . .

11. Arbitration is sometimes useful where the parties . . .

12. This point has troubled many courts . . .

13. Because he was injured . . .

Exercise 4

1. Appellant's opening brief contains three misstatements of fact.
2. The witness need not sign the deposition transcript until the errors are corrected.
3. In approving a class action settlement, the court must guard the interests of absent class members.
4. We cannot tell whether trial counsel's misconduct influenced the jury verdict.
5. We served our first set of interrogatories nine weeks ago.

Exercise 5

We turn now to plaintiff's request for an injunction. The defendant argues that an injunction is unnecessary, because the exclusionary clause is already void under this court's prior order. Since the exclusionary clause can have no further effect, the defendant argues that we can give the plaintiff complete relief without an injunction. Defendant's argument has obvious merit. Thus we have decided not to issue an injunction.

Exercise 6

1. Section 1038 pertains to any contract that provides for attorney fees.
2. Discovery can commence before the judge considers the motion.
3. We agree with your position, but if you intend to cause delay, we will oppose you.
4. To improve downstream water quality, we must stop polluting the headwaters.
5. If this breach continues, my client will terminate the contract immediately.
6. We could amend the interrogatory answer, but if we do so now, the court may suspect our client's good faith.
7. This court cannot fulfill the testator's wishes unless it invalidates the *inter vivos* transfer.
8. We seek to cooperate with you, and we hope that you will change your position. If you refuse to do so, and if you do not complete the work on schedule, we will impound your funds.

Exercise 7

1. An attorney who receives clients' funds must put them in the Client Trust Account.

2. Either party may terminate this agreement by giving thirty days notice to the other party.

3. Each month the defendant manufacturers exchanged price lists, and they agreed to make all sales at list price or above.

4. If my husband does not survive me by thirty days, I give my children such items of my personal property as my executor may select for them.

5. The supplier insisted that the goods were of merchantable quality.

6. In some cases you must fill out Form 242A before we can clear you through customs. We will not clear you through customs until the Immigration Officer approves your Form 242A. If the Immigration Officer decides that you do not need to fill out Form 242A, then we will clear you through customs promptly.

Exercise 8

1. Class actions serve an important function in our judicial system. They permit claims of many individuals to be resolved at the same time. This avoids repetitious litigation and gives claimants a way to enforce claims that are too small for individual litigation.

2. Consumers are sometimes abused and exploited by false, misleading, or irrelevant advertising. But that does not necessarily require the government to intrude into the marketplace. Consumers themselves can go to court, as can competing

sellers who lose business because of such advertising.

3. The majority opinion ignores an important fact: the states are sovereigns, both in common law and in federal constitutional law. Therefore, claims made by states are not generally subject to legal doctrines such as laches, acquiescence, estoppel, or statutes of limitations of the type in issue here.

Exercise 9

1. A response must be filed with the hearing officer within twenty days after the petition is served.
2. The attorney-client privilege applies to the client's revelation of a past crime. But it does not apply when the client seeks the attorney's aid to plan or carry out a future crime.
3. The sole eyewitness saw the accident from a seventh floor window, half a block north of the intersection. She testified that she did not see which car entered the intersection first.
4. Plaintiff's grandfather, Jose Cruz, later transferred the disputed 200 acres by a deed of gift which was bitterly contested by the heirs but which was ultimately upheld by the probate court.

Exercise 10

1. Appellant must have recognized the weakness of its claim. It was represented by Bishop & Donald,

counsel of long experience in government contract litigation, a field that requires no small degree of expertise.

2. The Model Rules of Professional Conduct require an attorney to deposit all funds received on behalf of a client in the attorney's client trust fund account. This duty does not apply to advances for attorney fees not yet earned, despite the danger that such advances may be misused.

Exercise 11

Unless the claim is framed as a federal question, venue would be proper in any of these judicial districts:

a. the Southern District of New York, if the plaintiff resides there; *or*
b. the Eastern District of California, if the defendant does business there; *or*
c. the Northern District of Illinois, if the events in question took place there.

Exercise 12

1. Only expensive therapy can alleviate plaintiff's pain.
2. The attorney argued that his client, being ignorant of the law, should receive a light sentence.

3. Defendant's argument overlooks a 1984 amendment to the statute.

4. Only when the claim is brought without good faith can attorney fees be awarded under Section 309.

5. The special tax provision was apparently intended, in the eyes of Congress, to encourage the production of cotton.

Exercise 13

1. The defendant International Business Machines Corporation is here called "IBM."

A simpler way is to show the abbreviation in parentheses after the proper name is used the first time: "Defendant International Business Machines (IBM) contracted with plaintiff. . . ."

2. One thing the Parole Board must consider is the prisoner's ability to get used to freedom.

3. The purpose of paragraph 9(f) is unclear, but it seems to have been included as an extra precaution.

4. Prison reform depends partly on how much the public knows about what is happening in prisons.

5. The patent laws, which give a seventeen-year monopoloy on "making, using, or selling the invention," concern the same general subject as the antitrust laws, and the two should be construed together. The patent laws modify the antitrust laws to some extent. That is why *General Electric* was decided as it was.

Exercise 14

1. All advance payments of rent under this lease will be binding on the lessor's successors.

2. Tenant has done nothing which would give anyone a claim against the leased premises. [This exercise and the answer are taken from Hathaway, *An Overview of the Plain English Movement for Lawyers*, 62 Mich. Bar J. 945 (1983).]

3. It is a misdemeanor for any person to spit in a public place.

4. It is a misdemeanor for any person to offer anything of value to an umpire, referee, judge, director, or supervisor of a sporting event with the intent to influence the outcome of the sporting event.

Exercise 15

1. The Privacy Act of 1974 says that each federal agency that asks you for information must tell you the following:

   - its legal right to ask for the information and whether the law says that you must give it;
   - what purpose the agency has in asking you for it and the use to which it will be put; and
   - what could happen if you do not give it.

[This exercise and the answer are taken from *Fine Print*, p. 1 (Jan. 1980). *Fine Print* is now published under the title *Simply Stated* by the Document Design Center of the American Institutes for Research, Washington, D.C. *Simply Stated* is an excellent newsletter for anyone interested in plain English.]

2. (a) Seminar on efficient management of law offices.

   (b) Regulations concerning bank accounts maintained by attorneys for client trust funds.

   (c) Presumptions affecting the burden of proof based on cost analysis.

3. Except as provided in Rule 9.3, any practitioner who is admitted in the highest court of a sister state shall be admitted to the bar of this court *pro hace vice,* upon motion by a member who is admitted to practice in this jurisdiction.

4. In an emergency, you will hear a loud horn. Go to the nearest stairs, and do what the Floor Captain tells you.

5. (a) Exposure to asbestos dust can cause grave injury or death.

   (b) Defendant's recklessness was caused by his callous disregard for the safety of his fellow workers.

   (c) Right after any industrial catastrophe that injures or kills many victims, a flock of plaintiffs' personal injury lawyers will swoop down like buzzards.

6. (a) Even the most honest witness will embellish the story unless you are in control at every moment of the questioning.

   (b) As a trial lawyer, you must develop your own

ways to deal with the witness who gives nonresponsive answers to your questions.

(c) All witnesses must be cautioned before giving their testimony that they are to listen carefully to the questions and that they are to answer only the questions that have been asked.

Additional Exercises

Exercise 1A

In each sentence below, underline the working words. Then rewrite the sentence, underline the working words, and compare your results with the original.

1. We believe that the conclusion that emerges in the light of this history is that every presumption should be on the side of the preservation of rights granted by the common law.

2. On the assumption that there is an absence of statutory language which would lead us to a contrary conclusion, it is our belief that preservation of rights to which the parties have become entitled under common law is the course of action most consistent with sound social policy.

3. It is the fact that heroin totaling one hundred grams and cocaine totaling fifty grams were discovered by the agents at the time of the arrest of the appellant.

4. This fact, standing alone, however, fails to compel one to reach the conclusion that there existed probable cause for the agents to believe that use had been made of the van owned by appellant for the transportation across state lines of the said heroin and cocaine.

Exercise 2A

Rewrite these sentences, omitting surplus words and avoiding compound constructions.

1. With respect to plaintiff's third claim, namely that there was a breach of warranty, the lower court held that by reason of the Uniform Commercial Code, which was applicable with reference to the sale, there could be no recovery.

2. The testimony of an economist, Dr. Bronovski, was offered for the purpose of undercutting plaintiff's evidence with respect to injury by reason of lost sales.

3. In order to prevail on a motion for summary judgment, the defendants must make a clear showing in terms of the lack of disputed issues of fact.

4. In reference to the allegations set forth in Paragraph 13, please identify by means of the date, author's name, and recipient's name, all laboratory reports written subsequent to June 29, 1984, but prior to February 25, 1985, in connection with studies conducted for the purpose of ascertaining the chemical composition of the allegedly infringing compounds.

5. From the point of view of judicial economy, defendant's petition should be denied in accordance with the principle that interlocutory appeals are disfavored. In the event that the defendant ulti-

mately loses at trial, it can appeal at that point in time with a view to challenging the trial judge's ruling, inasmuch as no prejudice is suffered prior to the time of entry of a final judgment.

Exercise 3A

Revise these sentences to omit the word-wasting idioms.

1. At that point in time, the deputies were not conducting a "search," even though it is the fact that they were looking through the windows of the car.

2. This is an instance in which Federal Rule of Evidence 803 would allow the admission of public records, insofar as they are relevant.

3. It is certainly not the case that every union political activity can escape scrutiny simply because of the fact that the First Amendment protects free speech.

4. It is of equal importance in this instance that the employees should not be able to secure the benefits of the contract for the period of the strike, until such time as they are willing also to accept the burdens thereof.

5. There is no doubt but that the inspector was justified by the obvious nervousness of the skipper in this case in demanding that the cargo be opened for further examination of its contents in an effort to answer the question as to whether there was contraband aboard.

6. In the case of a taxpayer who intentionally fails to report the item as income, this is an instance in which criminal prosecution would be appropriate.

7. If the situation is that the employer has made good faith efforts to comply with the statutory requirements, that should surely be considered, because it is not the case that the Department must prosecute *every* offender.

8. In the instance at hand, if attorney Lutz was aware of the fact that Ms. Bowles was employed in the Sales Division of the adversary corporation, then it was a situation in which he should have obtained consent of adversary counsel before interviewing her with respect to matters in connection with the litigation.

Exercise 4A

Rewrite these sentences, omitting surplus words and focusing on the actor, the action, and the object of the action.

1. There were four grounds stated in the *Perault* case for ordering the involuntary partition.

2. Since the purchase money has been delivered, it is now the appropriate time for us to close the escrow account.

3. Absent a claim of fraud, there is no way for plaintiff to avoid the plain language of the statute.

4. It is difficult for us to imagine a clearer case of abuse of process.

5. It is obvious that there is no factual basis for the second cause of action, and there is apparently no doubt but that plaintiff's attorneys realized that.

Exercise 5A

In the following passage you will find all the kinds of surplus words discussed in Chapter Two. Rewrite the passage, omitting as many surplus words as you can.

With respect to the use of evidence in regards to a person's character, there are certain basic principles that are familiar ground for each and every trial lawyer.

First, in the case of litigation which is concerned with civil claims, evidence relating to a person's character is not admissible when offered for the purpose of proving in what manner the said person acted on a particular occasion. Pursuant to this rule, should driver D cause the death of pedestrian P by driving over P, the plaintiff in a civil action charging D with the wrongful death of P could not introduce evidence about or concerning D's character in regards to driving in a wild manner as proof of how D drove on the occasion in question.

Second, in respect to litigation involving charges of violations of the criminal law, the general rule recited above is likewise applied, excluding situations in which certain statutes and rules have created exceptions with regard to instances in which the general rule is not applied. Thus, supposing it to be the case that in the example described above, driver D were charged with vehicular manslaughter in connection with the death of pedestrian P. By application of the general rule, evidence offered in the prosecution's case-in-chief for the purpose of proving D's character as respects wild driving would not be admissible as circumstantial proof of the manner in which D drove on the occasion in question.

Exercise 6A

Rewrite this paragraph of a judicial opinion, omitting surplus words and using base verbs in place of nominalizations.

Plaintiff bases its next argument on its contention that this case should be governed by a rule of *per se* illegality. With respect to some categories of restraints on trade, the courts have reached the conclusion that application of a *per se* rule is appropriate. In the situations to which a *per se* rule is applied, it is the intention of the courts to foreclose the defendant from any contention that the restraint of trade is reasonable in the circumstances. The *per se* rule has a tendency to operate unfairly in those instances where justification of the restraint may be found in economic efficiencies the achievement of which would be an impossibility in the absence of the restraint. We have reached the conclusion that justice would be ill served by application of a *per se* rule to the case at hand.

Exercise 7A

Rewrite these sentences, omitting surplus words, using base verbs instead of nominalizations, and using the active voice. Supply any missing information that you need.

1. If undue risk is to be avoided in your law practice, it must be remembered that attorney malpractice suits are becoming increasingly common, and ample malpractice insurance is regarded as a necessity by most prudent lawyers.

2. The jurors should be respected by attorneys, but undue solicitude should be avoided. An attorney's posture of fawning deference or attempts to curry favor are resented by jurors.

3. Within three days after a Preliminary Notice of Default has been filed by Owner, cancellation of all outstanding credit vouchers shall be made by Lender or Lender's agents.

4. Good faith efforts to purge the contempt by respondent shall be taken into consideration by the court when the sentence is set.

5. If no request for legal services has been made, and if the proposal of legal representation is made initially by the lawyer, the solicitation rule may have been violated.

6. The line which was drawn by ABA Model Rule 7.3 is not the same as the First Amendment line that

was drawn in the lawyer solicitation cases decided by the United States Supreme Court.

7. Initiation of personal contact with a potential client by a lawyer is prohibited by ABA Model Rule 7.3 in those instances in which the primary motivation for the initiation of personal contact is the lawyer's hope of personal financial gain.

Exercise 8A

Rewrite these passages using short sentences and omitting as many surplus words as you can.

1. In this law library there is hereafter to be no smoking, except in the lounge on the third floor which has been specifically set aside for that purpose, and there is to be no consumption of either food or drink in any portion of the law library, however eating and drinking are permitted in the snack bar area located in the basement.

2. Seeking to support the judgment on additional grounds not passed on by the Court of Appeals, but which have been argued here both orally and in the briefs, as was proper by reason of the fact that these grounds raise only issues of law and do not call for examination or appraisal of evidence, respondents assert that the contracts were in violation of the Wages and Hours Act.

3. Upon consideration of the motion made by plaintiff in the above entitled action to compel the defendant herein to answer certain questions posed to her at a deposition properly noticed and taken

in the within action, and upon consideration of the defendant's opposition thereto, and having heard the arguments of counsel in open court, and having considered the entire record on file herein, and having concluded that the deposition questions in issue are relevant to the within action, or are likely to lead to the discovery of admissible evidence, and are not objectionable on the ground that they call for information that would be protected by any privilege granted by statute or the common law, it is, therefore

ORDERED AND DECREED that plaintiff's motion be, and hereby is, granted; and it is further

ORDERED AND DECREED that defendant shall appear and answer the deposition questions which are the subject of the said motion at a date to be set by mutual agreement of counsel for the plaintiff and counsel for the defendant herein; and it is further

ORDERED AND DECREED that defendant shall pay to plaintiff the sum of $1,000, said amount reflecting costs and a reasonable attorney fee incurred by plaintiff in pursuing the above motion as aforesaid.

Exercise 9A

Close the gaps in each sentence by moving the intervening words or by splitting the sentence into two. When you rewrite, omit surplus words.

1. Plaintiff's complaint, containing nine causes of action including slander, invasion of privacy, intentional interference with prospective business advantage, and intentional infliction of emotional distress, was filed last Tuesday.

2. Intentional interference with prospective business advantage, although related to a more familiar tort known generally by the name interference with contract, or intentional interference with contractual relations, or inducement of breach of contract, does not require proof that the defendant interfered with a presently existing contract.

3. Plaintiff's intentional interference claim alleges, in language typical of the lawyers in the firm of Hungerdunger, Hungerdunger, & Hungerdunger who are serving as plaintiff's counsel and who are known throughout this jurisdiction for the pureleness, as well as the opacity of their prose, business losses of one million dollars.

4. Our best line of defense against the intentional interference claim, which is not defective on its face but which has absolutely no basis in fact, is promptly to take the deposition of the plaintiff and then to make, using the admissions that we will undoubtedly be able to extract from the plaintiff, a motion for partial summary judgment.

Exercise 10A

Rewrite these sentences without the nested modifiers. As you rewrite, omit surplus words.

1. Medical insurance, which in the case of union members is covered by a five year contract hammered out a few months ago through collective bargaining, is among the company's most generous fringe benefits.

2. Computation of the amount to be entered on line 23 can be accomplished by subtracting the amount entered on line 14, which is obtained by adding the amounts on lines 5, 6 (but not more than $1,000), and 7, from the amount entered on line 22.

Exercise 11A

Use tabulation to clarify this passage. When you rewrite it, omit surplus words.

If you have accrued 5 years of service in the home office, or 3 years of service in a field office, excluding, however, a field office located within 20 miles of your permanent residence; or, if you have served not less than 2 out of the most recent 4 years in an overseas office (except the overseas offices in Paris, Madrid, and Bonn) and were not accompanied by your dependents, you are eligible for the Paid Leave of Absence Program; excepting, however, executive officers (Pay Scale EX-6 or above), clerical employees (Pay Scale C-8 or below), and persons not qualified for Section A benefits.

Exercise 12A

Rewrite these sentences to solve the modifier problems. If a sentence has more than one possible meaning, select whichever one you wish and rewrite the sentence to express that meaning unambiguously.

1. Being constantly alert for signs of mechanical or dynamic injury, the deceased is examined by the pathologist to determine the cause of death.
2. A skilled pathologist is able to distinguish between structural changes produced by trauma and those produced by disease through years of training and experience.
3. In gunshot cases, a determination must be made whether the wound was inflicted before or after death by the pathologist.
4. Because of lack of mass and velocity, the pathologist will usually have difficulty with projectiles fired by small caliber pistols.
5. A pathologist can express an educated guess only on the probable cause of death.

Exercise 13A

Rewrite these passages using familiar, concrete words and omitting surplus words.

1. Judgment upon any arbitration award which may be rendered herein may be entered in any court having jurisdiction thereof.

2. The within Agreement constitutes the entire understanding and agreement between the Parties hereto with respect to the subject matter hereof, and no modification or amendment hereof shall be valid or binding upon the Parties hereto unless said modification or amendment is made in writing and signed on behalf of each of the said Parties by their respective proper officers thereunto duly authorized.

3. Defendant, having been interrupted *in flagrante delicto*, can hardly be heard to assert that his conduct was not the *causa causans* of the injury.

4. NOW THEREFORE, BE IT KNOWN that in consideration of the premises as well as in consideration of the sum of Five Thousand Dollars ($5,000.00) paid in hand by Licensee to Licensor contemporaneously with the delivery by Licensor to Licensee of a duly executed copy of this License Agreement, and in consideration of the royalty payments herein specified to be paid by Licensee to Licensor, and in consideration of the terms, conditions, and covenants herein set forth, it is mutually agreed and covenanted by and between Licensor and Licensee as follows, to wit:

5. It is my desire and intention to give and provide to my beloved step-daughter, the said Angelina, a full and complete education, including post-graduate training if that be her interest, wish and desire. I do therefore hereby give, devise, and bequeath unto her, to have and to hold, all my right, title, and

interest in and to the following properties described hereinbelow:

Exercise 14A

When you rewrite the following passages, pay special attention to your choice of words.

1. Every person who unlawfully throws out a switch, removes a rail, or places any obstruction on any railroad with the intention of derailing any passenger, freight, or other train, car, or engine, or who unlawfully places any dynamite or other explosive material or any other obstruction upon or near the track of any railroad with the intention of blowing up or derailing any such train, car, or engine, or who unlawfully sets fire to any railroad bridge or trestle, over which any such train, car, or engine must pass with the intention of wrecking such train, car, or engine, is guilty of a felony, and shall be punished by imprisonment in the state prison for life without possibility of parole.

2. Advertisers are hereby notified that it is the policy of this newspaper to refuse publication of any material designed for the purpose of encouraging, promoting, influencing, or advancing the sale of any products, wares, goods, commodities, services, or the like, which because of its content, form, style, substance, appearance, or manner of presentation is or may be likely to cause any reader thereof to believe that said material is an article, story, col-

umn, editorial, or similar non-advertising portion of this newspaper.

Exercise 15A

1. Rewrite this passage to eliminate the elegant variation:

> An attorney is subject to professional discipline for incompetence. Proceedings to impose professional sanction may be taken against practitioners who undertake matters they know they are not sufficiently skilled to handle. Further, lawyers who accept a case and then fail to prepare to handle the matter in an able manner can be censured, suspended, or disbarred. Not only attorney discipline but also civil liability for malpractice must be taken into consideration. In actions for professional negligence, lawyers can be held liable for damages proximately caused by their incompetence. Plaintiffs in legal malpractice litigation include not only clients, but also other persons who were intended to benefit from the services rendered by the defendant practitioner.

2. Eliminate the multiple negatives in this passage:

> It shall be a violation of these rules for any member to fail to post a notice in a prominent place that is not obscured from public view listing the member's retail prices for all items offered for sale, excepting only limited time special sale prices offered for not more than three days.

3. The following passage is from a bulletin written by an in-house
   lawyer for a corporation. The purpose of the bulletin is to inform the corporation's employees about a new legal service
   plan. When you rewrite the passage, avoid cosmic detachment by addressing it directly to the employees, and make the
   passage as simple and easy to read as you can:

   > Entitlement to participation in the Employee Legal
   > Service Plan is dependent upon the employee's com-
   > pliance with the following requirements: (a) employ-
   > ment with the company must have commenced at
   > least thirty (30) days prior to enrollment by the em-
   > ployee in the Plan; (b) employment must be on a Reg-
   > ular Staff basis, the Plan not being available to any
   > person employed on either a Casual or Temporary
   > Help basis; and (c) the employee must have submit-
   > ted a completed Employee Legal Service Plan Enroll-
   > ment Form to Personnel & Employment Services, and
   > an appropriate Payroll Deduction Request must have
   > been filed by the employee with Accounting & Payroll.

4. The following passage is from a book intended for lawyers who
   wish to work on the legal staff of a corporation. Revise it to
   eliminate the sexist language:

   > The function of inhouse corporate counsel in admin-
   > istering litigation is sometimes said to be limited: His
   > job is to achieve the best practical results at the low-
   > est reasonable cost. He has done his work well if he
   > selects the best man as outside trial counsel, and then
   > reviews the matter from time to time to make sure
   > things are proceeding on course. That view is un-
   > sound for many reasons. The trial lawyer is an im-
   > portant link between the corporation and the public;
   > frequently he is called on to respond in the heat of

battle with little or no notice. Generally his interests and perceptions are far different from the corporate executive, the man who lives daily within the corporation. The outside trial lawyer may be an expert in trial strategy, tactics, and practice, but he is almost certainly no expert in corporate management and policy. Inhouse corporate counsel need not have had trial experience to manage litigation, though it helps if he has earned his spurs in a few years of law firm practice. But it is important that he know enough about litigation to handle policy decisions, judge the effectiveness of trial counsel, and administer those matters which are his primary responsibility.

At that point in time, useless
compound construction,
11
Average sentence length, how
to measure, 34–35; 74n

Bad construction, how to spot
it, 7–10
Base verbs, 23–24
Basis, as an abstraction, 51
Bates v. *State Bar of Arizona,*
cited, 51
Bernstein, T., cited, 74n, 76n
Bequeath, devise and give,
lawyer's tautology, 18–21
Boilerplate, 4
By means of, useless
compound construction,
11
By reason of, useless
compound construction,
11
By virtue of, useless
compound construction,
11

California Plain English
Statute, cited, 73n
California Penal Code § 631
(a), quoted, 31–32
Cardozo, B., quoted, 5
Cardozo, B., writing style
characteristics, 5–6
Case, spawns verbosity, 13–14
Cease and Desist, a lawyer's
tautology, 18–21
Chains of nouns, a language
quirk, 61
Change or alter, lawyer's
tautology, 18–21

Character and kind, lawyer's
tautology, 18–21
Choppiness, need for variety
in sentence length,
34–35
Circumstances, as an
abstraction, 51
Clarity,
guide to clarity in sentence
construction, 34–35
influence of word order on,
44–46
lack of in lawyers' writing
style, 3
loss of caused by elegant
variation, 59–60
need to avoid passive voice,
27–29
served by use of familiar
words, 52–53
short sentences aid, 31–35
use of active voice to
obtain, 27–29
Clear and free, lawyer's
tautology, 18–21
Clearly, a throat clearer, 67
Clemens, S., quoted, 35
Clusters of words, common
clusters that cause
verbosity, 12–14
Collins, R., cited, 76n
Collins & Hattenhauer, cited,
73n
Commentary, use of strong
nouns and verbs for,
64–65
Common law lawyers,
writing style of
transplanted to
America, 3

Book and cover design/Robert Maddock, Left
Hand Graphics
Artwork/Jan Conroy
Wordwork/Arlene Snyder